THE WORLD OF
VISUAL
ILLUSIONS

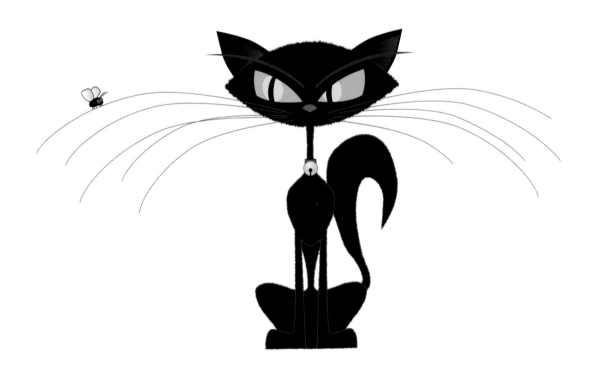

THE WORLD OF VISUAL ILLUSIONS

OPTICAL TRICKS THAT DEFY BELIEF!

GIANNI A. SARCONE AND MARIE-JO WAEBER

ARCTURUS

ARCTURUS

This edition published in 2012 by Arcturus Publishing Limited
26/27 Bickels Yard, 151–153 Bermondsey Street,
London SE1 3HA

Copyright © 2012 Arcturus Publishing Limited/Gianni A. Sarcone &
Marie-Jo Waeber

All rights reserved. No part of this publication may be reproduced,
stored in a retrieval system, or transmitted, in any form or by any means,
electronic, mechanical, photocopying, recording or otherwise, without
prior written permission in accordance with the provisions of the
Copyright Act 1956 (as amended). Any person or persons who do any
unauthorised act in relation to this publication may be liable to criminal
prosecution and civil claims for damages.

ISBN: 978-1-84858-664-2
AD002102EN

Printed in Singapore

CONTENTS

INTRODUCTION

'There is not enough darkness in all the world to put out the light of even one small candle.'

Robert Alden

Roughly 14 billion years ago, the universe originated in a cosmic light explosion. Ten billion years later the planet we call Earth gave birth to life, which eventually led to our modern human civilization. The probability of that sequence of events is absolutely infinitesimal, and yet it still happened. Dear reader, you are lucky to be here!

There is a strange analogy between the world globe and the globe of the human eye. The thin film of gases that surrounds the Earth – the atmosphere – is able to capture and absorb solar radiation; likewise, the thin film of neurons that covers the back of the eyeball, called the retina, catches and records the light and thus the images from the outer world; both films separate the visible from the darkness. It is said that the eye is the jewel of the head, and like a jewel it is a very effective light trap. Our eye can detect, under right conditions, the flicker of a small candle between up to 15 km (9 miles) away!

Over millions of years, the human eye (and indirectly the visual system) has slowly modified itself, becoming the privileged instrument of a mammal that ceased to use its nose to comprehend the world and began to rely on its vision. The ability to discern red from green helped our ancestors to forage for food: it was important to distinguish red-ripe, nutritious fruits from leaves. Apart from humans and a small group of primates, only a few animals can see colours – fish, amphibians and some birds. While most animals do not care much about the substance of things, tending instead to care 'where things go', we humans are concerned about 'what and how things are'. Our eyes move rapidly and jerkily, yet we are very skilled in detecting small objects: we are more concerned by still images than movement.

THE PATHWAY TO THE BRAIN

Although light shines through the eye pupil and lens like a projector, casting an image on the back wall, our eyeball is much more than a tiny cinema. The eye's movie screen – or retina – is made up of thousands of nerve cells able to detect light and, above all, capable of channelling these visual signals into the coordinating centre of sensation that is the brain via a chain of electro-chemical events similar to a domino reaction. Imagine the incredible number of nerve cells receiving visual impulses from any single eye and passing them on to the next neurons by making sure that the correct impulse continues on its path.

Indeed, what we see depends mainly on the brain; it uses the electro-chemical signals received from the eyes to make sense of what is seen. But it also adds extra ingredients of its

own – attention, memory and meaning. It is because of these that on occasion you apparently see something that does not represent reality; everything you observe is affected by the context, your prior knowledge, and your inbuilt assumptions. Even the manner in which you look at things dramatically affects your perception of them. When differences occur between your perceptions or expectations and the image seen, you are experiencing an optical illusion, and scientists have been studying these for centuries in order to understand how the brain works.

The authors of this book are leading authorities on visual perception and designers of optical illusions that fascinate neuroscientists worldwide, and here you will find many new artworks that have been created during their optical illusion workshops. *The World of Visual Illusions* provides an exciting approach to a well-established subject, placing the emphasis on interaction, education and creative thinking; it is divided up into nine chapters, each one featuring numerous illusory types such as size distortions, hidden figures, moving patterns, colour adaptations and many more. The illusions will fascinate, challenge and trick you, and the explanations of how they work will encourage you to look differently at the world we live in.

CHAPTER 1

EVERYDAY ILLUSIONS

'Nothing is exactly as it seems, nor is it otherwise.'
Alan Watts (1915–73)

At some point in our lives, most of us have walked under the stars with a lover and, admiring the immensity of the night sky sprinkled with light, have made everlasting promises ... too bad that all this was an illusion, because most of the stars in the sky have not existed for centuries. What we see of stars is not what they currently are, but what they were; we are so far away that it takes years for the light that they give off to become visible to us.

We are so confident in believing what we see, because it is usually the right response in order to survive – but nature offers a lot of unbelievable illusions that often pass unnoticed or unconsidered because we see them every day.

These 'natural' illusions are of two kinds: *physical illusions* and *physiological illusions*. The former are naturally occurring phenomena observable by any person with proper vision, such as refraction (when a spoon in a glass of water appears broken or bent), the illusion that the moon looks larger when rising and setting,

a rainbow, a mirage, or the moiré pattern. We may include in this category illusions that result from our (or our camera's) point of view.

On the other hand, physiological illusions are due to the conformation of the eye and also to the effects on it of prolonged stimulation of a specific type such brightness, tilt, colour, movement, and so on. Some common illusions in this category are the afterimage, the aftereffect and the contrast effect. In both categories of natural illusions, we may include colours (yes, colour only starts to exist when our perception systems translate this electromagnetic phenomenon into the impression of 'colour').

In nature, some animals even play visual tricks – which we often refer to as the 'art of camouflage' – to escape from predators or to aid them in hunting their prey.

In the following pages, you will find several examples that will help you to understand why your brain sometimes misinterprets the messages it receives from your eyes.

BLURRED FACES

In the upper picture, you can see the blurred face of a woman and beside it one in sharp focus. Stare at the fixation star between these two faces for about 20–30 seconds, then *quickly* look at the fixation star of the lower picture.

You will notice that just for a few seconds the image of the woman on the right appears to be more blurred than the left one, though in fact they are perfectly identical. The illusion comes from a visual aftereffect that scientists call 'contrast adaptation' or 'contrast gain control'. This experiment shows that prolonged exposure to blurred, or unfocused, images influences visual acuity and contrast sensitivity.

Figure A

Figure B

green zone

blue zone

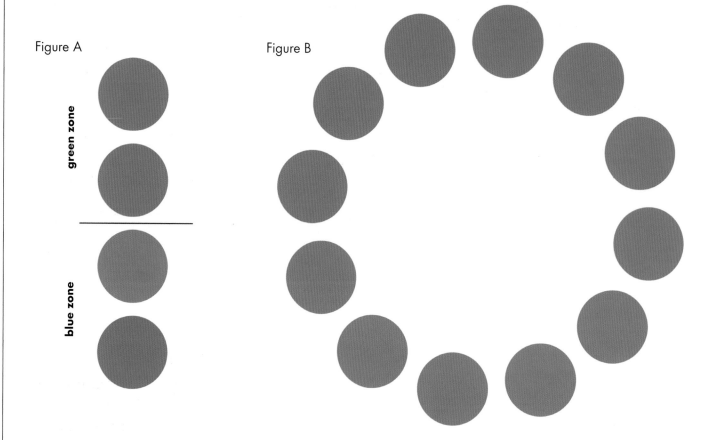

WHEN GREEN BECOMES BLUE

Different cultures have different terms for colours, and may even assign some colour terms to slightly different parts of the colour spectrum. For instance, Italian distinguishes blue (*blu*) and royal blue (*azzurro*); in Japan, although the traffic lights use the same colours as in other countries, the green light is described by the same word as blue (*aoi*), because green is considered to be a shade of blue. How colours are categorized is a subjective decision that depends on language and perception, not a matter of immutable fact.

To test this for yourself, try the following experiment. In Fig. A you can see that it's easy to divide a blue-green colour-gradient set of plates into two colour categories – but if you ask your friends to divide the circular set of colour plates in Fig. B into sectors each containing blue or green plates, everyone will come up with a different solution.

SINGING JEANS

Because of the innate human tendency to impose a pattern on ambiguous shapes, this amusing anthropomorphic photograph may be seen to represent a blues singer. Scientists call this phenomenon 'pareidolia'. In fact, to identify an object, our brain matches what we see against our stored knowledge, experiences and, sometimes, expectations. Under clinical circumstances, some psychologists encourage pareidolia as a means to gain insight into a person's mental state: the famous Rorschach inkblot test is used for that purpose.

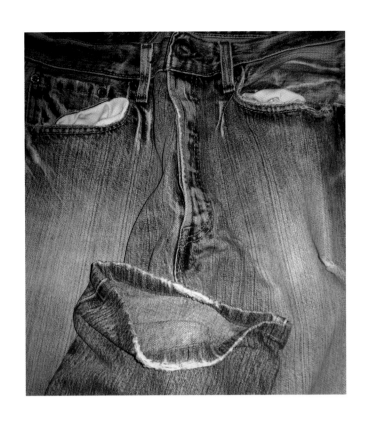

FLOATING SAUSAGE

Point your index fingers towards each other and hold them near the bridge of your nose, at eye level, as illustrated in the upper picture. Leave just a short space between your two index fingers and focus on something a few meters (yards) away. You should now see a short 'sausage' floating in between your two index fingers (see lower picture). If you are having problems seeing it, try moving your fingers slowly away from your eyes – the 'sausage' should appear at some point. This illusion is a kind of natural stereogram.

Figure A

SCINTILLATING MAZE

Take a look at this maze (Fig. A), shifting your gaze around it. Dark dots will seem to suddenly twinkle and vanish at the crossings of the horizontal and vertical paths that form the maze. This kind of physiological illusion is presumed to be the aftermath on the eyes or brain from excessive visual stimulation or interaction with competing visual stimuli of a specific type (brightness, position, size, and so on). It's believed that in the early stages of visual processing those specific visual stimuli have individual dedicated neural channels. When only one or a few channels have continual stimulation, a physiological imbalance develops that consequently alters perception. This illusion, first reported by Ludimar Hermann in 1870, is named the 'Hermann grid illusion'.

In the variation in Fig. B, the dots that appear seem even brighter.

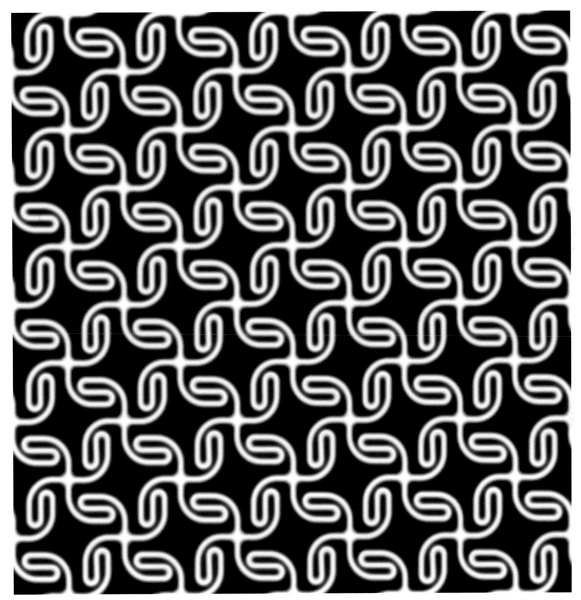

Figure B

SCALE MODEL ILLUSIONS

The 'tilt-shift' or 'Playmobil' effect is a process by which a location (or object) in a photograph is made to look like a miniature scale model. It is done by blurring parts of the photograph to simulate the shallow depth of field encountered in macro (close-up) photography, making the scene seem much smaller than it actually is. You can do the blurring either optically (when you take the photograph), or by digital post-processing.

When taking or choosing a photograph for the tilt-shift effect, bear in mind that miniature

In this manipulated photograph you can see a sporting event at Reser Stadium, Oregon, where the people look like tiny toy figurines.

models are usually viewed from above, so you should ideally use a photograph with an elevated viewpoint and a reasonably wide angle of view. With basic techniques and digital tools such as the mask mode, gradient and blur filter of image-editing software, you can blur any photograph so that only the subject remains sharp. If you do it correctly the effect will be quite similar to that obtained using lens tilt. Tilt-shift photography relies on the Scheimpflug principle, which is applied to correcting perspective distortion and focus in photographs.

Here the clock tower of Big Ben in London looks more like a cardboard scale model than the tall, imposing building it is in reality.

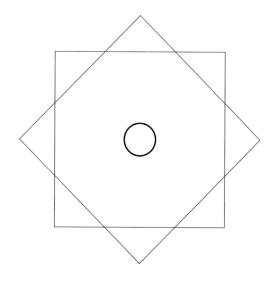

AFTERIMAGE RIVALRY

Fix the coloured diagram in your mind by looking at the fixation cross for about 40–50 seconds, then rapidly shift your gaze to the fixation disc within the white frames. If you concentrate on the diamond outline you will perceive the afterimage corresponding to it (red diamond), while if you study the square outline you will see a yellow square afterimage. With a little effort, you can shift which afterimage you experience by attending to one shape and then the other. You will also notice that the yellow square is the last afterimage to vanish. Curiously, some people report that when they stare steadily at the diagram, the green diamond disappears! This illusion is based on Peter Tse's 'attention-biased afterimage rivalry effect'.

EYESPOT MIMICRY

The cat in the picture is our best assistant. His name is Sylvester and he often frequents our studio because he has adopted a comfortable chair as his pied-à-terre.

If you stare for a while at the eyes of our sleeping assistant, don't you have the impression that his eyes open suddenly? The strange stripe pattern around his closed eyes (Fig. A) reproduces roughly the outlines of real cat eyes (Fig. B). Animals convey messages via their eyes, so these 'subjective eyes', called 'ocelli' by scientists, could be useful to scare off eventual predators during his sleep – but when he is awake they also make his eyes larger than they really are, like natural eyeliners. This kind of visual automimicry is similar to the 'eyespots' of some butterflies, such as *Smerinthus ocellatus* in Fig. C.

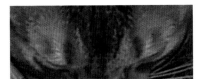

Figure A

Figure B

Figure C

LEVITATING ILLUSION

When objects on a surface are viewed from above, our brain correctly reads them as being in contact with that surface. However, when a shadow of their shape is painted beneath them, they appear to levitate. You can reproduce this levitating effect quite easily by adding shadows to a photograph.

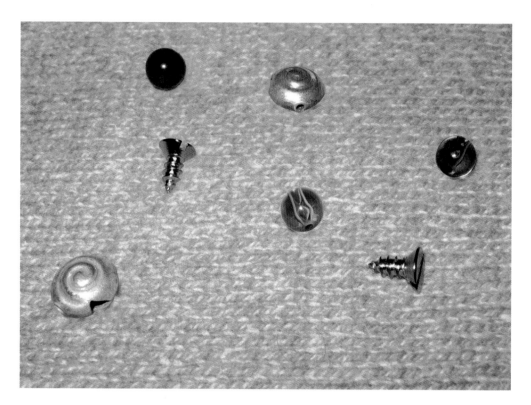

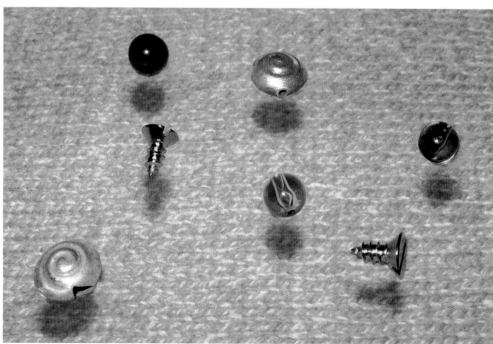

CONTINUOUS DIAGONALS?

Are some of the oblique lines in the picture continuous from one edge of the pattern to the other? No, but you have to take a closer look at the pattern in order to realize it is composed only of short intermittent segments. This shows that our eyes aren't able to immediately perceive simple details in a moderately large pattern. This novelty illusion was created by Gianni A. Sarcone.

CHAPTER 2

EARLY OPTICAL ILLUSIONS

'The great majority of mankind are satisfied with appearances, as though they were realities, and are often more influenced by the things that seem than by those that are.'

Niccolò Machiavelli (1469–1527)

Make-up was the first deliberate visual illusion to be used by our earliest ancestors, to make themselves look more desirable or more formidable, according to circumstances. There is no doubt that our ancestors were aware that optical illusions occur, even if they did not understand the physical or cerebral mechanisms that created them.

From the times of the earliest civilizations right up to the present day, artists, philosophers and scientists have attempted to assign explanations and meanings to the world that surrounds us and the way we interact with it. Optical illusions have played a constructive role in this search for 'truth' – it has been extremely useful to know how we can be fooled, increasing our understanding of how the human brain functions. As a result of discovering our limitations, we also created tools to extend our senses in ways which help us to comprehend the elements of the world that are not immediately apparent.

Architects, visual artists, designers, and decorators have all regularly used visual illusions to enhance the appearance of their creations. The idea of course is to produce a pleasant sensory quality in the object, painting or building. Sometimes the goal is to impress, confuse, or trick the observer by creating objects in space that seem larger or smaller than they really are – and of course set designers employ visual tricks to carry the audience's imagination to other environments and even distant countries. However, optical illusions have also been created for the sheer fun of playing tricks and for intellectual pleasure. They are useful to conjurors and con artists, too!

The ancient optical illusions shown in the following pages largely fit into one of four categories: hidden figures, multipart and composite figures, ambiguous and reversible figures, and distorted figures.

TWO-FACED MAN

Here is a particularly fascinating illusive Roman floor mosaic: a 'topsy-turvy head' inscribed in a circle bordered by a two-strand braid. Seen from one side it depicts a bald and bearded old man with dark shadows under the eyes, but when from the opposite side it shows a beardless young man with leonine hair.

The mosaic was found in a *triclinium* (dining room) of what was a *domus romana* (a Roman house) in the center of Ascoli Piceno, a town in the Marche region of Italy. Such reversible mosaics dating from the late Roman period are extremely rare, but in 2006 a similar mosaic was also found in the town of Pomezia, near Rome.

MAN OR MONSTER?

The charm of this very old topsy-turvy picture lies in its ability to represent a second picture altogether when it is turned upside down. The picture on the left depicts a rear view of a man kneeling down, while in the right-hand picture the man's braces and the heels of his shoes turn magically into the eyes and tusks of a grotesque figure.

PIRANESI'S GOTHIC PRISON

L'Arco Gotico ('The Gothic Arch') is plate XIV of a series of 16 prints made by the Italian artist Giambattista Piranesi. This collection of etchings called *Carceri d'invenzione* ('Imaginary Prisons') shows enormous subterranean vaults with sweeping staircases, towering arches and mighty machines. But something in this Gothic picture is wrong. In terms of perspective, the arch – which is in the background, emphasized in red – is incorrectly aligned with the lower part of the architectural structure in the foreground, also emphasized in red.

THE WIFE AND MOTHER-IN-LAW

Do you see the profile of a young lady or of an old one? If you observe the picture carefully, you will notice that the mother-in-law's nose is the young wife's chin; her mouth is the wife's necklace, and her eye is the wife's ear! This old illusion shows how our visual system tends to group features based upon what we expect to see.

This classic illusion, featured on a German postcard from 1888, was copied and adapted by hundreds of artists and psychologists throughout the 19th and 20th centuries, including the cartoonist William Ely Hill who published this picture in the magazine *Puck* in 1915 (Fig. A). Interesting variations on this illusion include the 'Husband and father-in-law' by Jack Botwinick (1961, Fig. B) and a French one called '*Où est sa grand-mère?*' (before 1900, Fig. C). This kind of illusion, where we experience two equally possible perceptions, is called a 'bistable illusion'.

Figure A

Figure B

Figure C

Society

A PORTRAIT.

A PORTRAIT OF SOCIETY

Look at this satirical etching by George A. Wotherspoon from a distance. Is this a well-dressed gentleman, escorting two ladies to a dance? Or maybe a donkey?

FACE IN THE LANDSCAPE

Find the hidden face in this engraving of a landscape by Johann Martin Will (1780). Here's a clue: turn the image 90 degrees clockwise.

HOGARTH'S PERSPECTIVES

One of the first artists to deliberately misuse perspective in order to create an impossible landscape was the English artist William Hogarth (1697–1764) whose artwork *Perspective Absurdities* formed the frontispiece to J. J. Kirby's book *Dr Brook Taylor's Method of Perspective Made Easy in both Theory and Practice* (1754), with the caption 'Whoever makes a design without the knowledge of perspective will be liable to such absurdities as are shown in this frontispiece'.

In the engraving there are 20 'absurdities'. For instance, the fisherman in the foreground has his line further out than the fisherman on the riverbank; the tiles the foreground fisherman stands on have a vanishing point that means they converge towards the viewer; the man on the hill seems as big as the woman lighting his pipe from the bedroom window; the pub's signboard is moored to two buildings, one in front of the other, and the church appears to front onto the river, but both its ends are visible at the same time! Aside from the impossibilities of scale there are approximately ten different horizons based on the various vanishing points.

GOSSIP

Where two women are gossiping the devil is not far away! This is another neat satirical etching by George A. Wotherspoon, which represents a menacing multipart face involving feminine figures. In this case, however, the message is not of a sexual nature but implies a veiled criticism of women's vanity. The two mirrored feminine figures in the foreground symbolize the reflection of the ego and are a manifestation of self-importance, or the triumph of appearance over substance.

LORDS OF THE LAND

In this English patriotic popular engraving from 1831 there are hidden profiles of William IV and Lords Grey, Brougham, Russell and Durham. Can you find them all?

SPOOKY EFFECTS

The book of afterimage effects called *Spectropia, or Surprising Spectral Illusions: Showing Ghosts Everywhere, and of any Colour* by J. H. Brown must have delighted its young audience when it was first published in 1863. The readers were asked to focus their attention on the various ghostly plates in the book, such as the one shown here, and then look at a blank wall. Try it for yourself: the spectre will vanish and reappear several times, and the colours of the plate will be reversed. The author concluded with a detailed explanation of the phenomenon of complementary afterimages and the persistence of vision.

WHERE IS THE DRIVER?

Find the driver in this puzzling picture taken from the children's book *Where Am I?* by Tatiana Glebova, published in Russia in 1928. If you can't spot him, you can see the solution on page 126.

CHAPTER 3

SPATIAL ILLUSONS

'Anyone who can handle a needle convincingly can make us see a thread which is not there'

Ernst Gombrich (1909–2001)

Inhabiting the flat surface of the Earth as we do, we are influenced by horizontal depth perspective: it is the reason why our eyes are aligned horizontally, not vertically. In fact, the different positions of the eyes mean that two slightly different projections of the world are produced on the retinas. This simple dual process, called 'stereopsis', leads to the perception of depth and also to interesting visual illusions and discoveries. The differences in the two retinal images are called 'horizontal disparity' or 'binocular disparity'.

In the context of perspective, near vision and far vision sometimes deliver contrasting messages, mainly due to the spherical nature of the eye. This means that in some cathedrals, for example, columns that are closer to the viewer may appear narrower than those far away because the angle of view means that the full diameter of the closer column is not visible (see Figure A). Since antiquity, clever subterfuges have been used in architecture to correct such

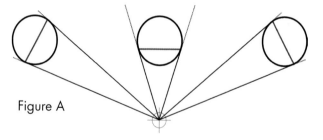

Figure A

paradoxical illusions. In fact, the Ancient Greeks introduced a technique known as 'entasis' which incorporates a slight convexity in the columns of temples to compensate for the illusion of concavity created by parallel straight shafts.

Over the centuries, scientists and artists have invented techniques to trick our visual depth perception. Counter-perspective and accelerated perspective techniques have been used to correct unpleasant perspectival distortions, while other artistic techniques and devices such as trompe-l'oeils, stereograms and anaglyphs that use perspective rules and visual vergence (convergence and divergence of the eyes) have simulated real-life three-dimensional scenes.

CREATING DEPTH WITH COLOURS

Colour directly affects the appearance of depth. If you look at this picture for a while, the coloured grids will appear to be distanced from each other and the whole picture will assume a three-dimensional aspect. On a solid black background, a red surface or structure is usually perceived as closer, while a blue one is seen as further away, a colour phenomenon known as 'chromostereopsis'.

RECURSIVE WATCH

The 'Drost effect' refers to a 'recursive' picture that depicts an infinite reduced version of itself in a place where a similar but realistic picture would be expected to appear. It can be compared to the visual experience of standing between two mirrors, seeing an infinite reproduction of one's image. To make the recursive watch shown in the picture, the photograph was cut into two distinct parts and then distorted to fit repeatedly into a logarithmic spiral, continuing this operation as long as the resolution of the picture would allow.

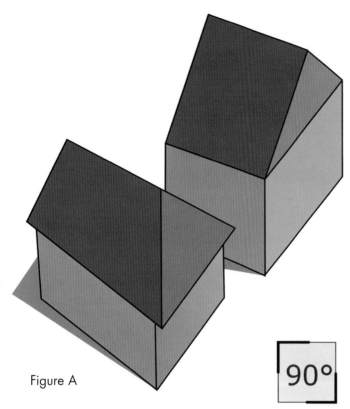

Figure A

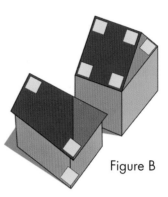

90°

HIDDEN RIGHT ANGLES

How many 90-degree angles are hidden in this 3D rendering (Fig. A)? The answer is eight! (See Fig. B). People usually manage to locate up to six right angles relatively easily, but a tough one to find is that on the upper side of the house in the background. Two or three of the 90-degree angles don't look very convincing, but this is entirely due to a trick of the apparent perspective.

Figure B

VISUAL LABYRINTHS

Now look at the three spiral labyrinths A, B, and C (Fig. A). Though they might appear the same, they present some fundamental differences. Which ant scuttling through its respective maze will finally reach the sugar cubes?

To find the answer, think of these decorative spiral designs as if they were rolled pastries. If we fill with red the paths that are actually only closed spaces, we can easily see that the labyrinth C shows a continuous double-spiral path that leads to the sugar cubes (Fig. B). If we test the other paths in A and B, we will soon discover that they are dead-ended (see the blue paths). The interlaced spirals in C are made with two rolled-up one-folded green layers, while the labyrinthine spirals in B and A are made with just one rolled-up green layer, folded respectively once (B) or twice (A).

These figures have been adapted from a visual test made by the psychologists Marvin L. Minsky and Seymour A. Papert.

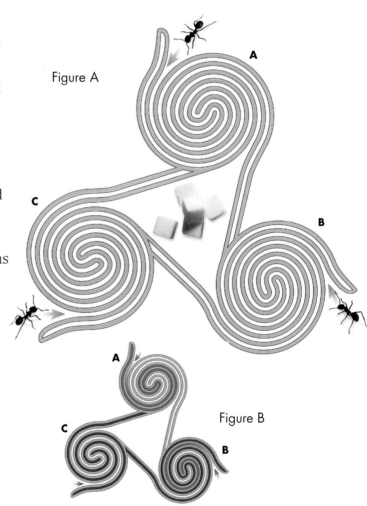

Figure A

Figure B

HOLBEIN'S AMBASSADORS

The Ambassadors is a double portrait of Jean de Dinteville, a landowner, and Georges de Selve, a bishop, painted by Hans Holbein the Younger in 1533. According to art critics, the anamorphic skull in the foreground of the picture may be a wordplay involving the artist's name, because in German a skull can be described as a *hohl Bein* which means a 'hollow bone'.

To make the skull appear in its recognizable form, tilt the book perpendicularly to your face and look at this picture from close to its right-hand side. You can also use the back of a tablespoon: place the spoon at the top right of the elongated skull in the middle of the painting with the back of the spoon perpendicular to the painting and pointing to the left.

THE ANNUNCIATION

Here is another example of misleading perspectival architecture.
This 15th-century fresco depicting the Annunciation was
discovered in the Grote Kerk of Breda in the Netherlands at the
beginning of the 20th century. It is one of the many unintentional
'impossible figure' paintings of the medieval era. In fact, the central
pillar that holds the two arcs has been painted behind the central
figures, though the two other pillars are in the foreground.

THE AMES ROOM

Although the boy here appears to be dramatically greater in height, the woman is actually taller. Additionally, although the room looks as if it is cubic, its real shape is quite different.

The 'Ames room' is a specially built room that appears normal because of the constancy of the size and shape of the squares. Actually, the walls (and some of the windows) are trapezoidal and one corner is much farther away from the observer than the other. When two people stand in the corners, one person looks small while the other appears a giant, and when a ball is rolled straight ahead, it appears to go uphill. Such illusions are related to forced perspective.

The Ames Room was perfected by American ophthalmologist Adelbert Ames (1880–1955) in 1946, based on a concept originally conceived in the late 19th century by Hermann L. von Helmholtz, a German scientist.

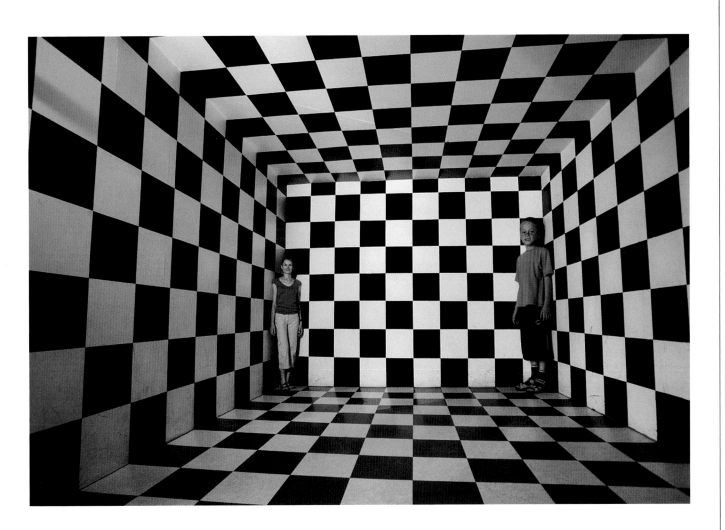

TWISTED IRON ROPES

Are all the cables perfectly straight and parallel to each other? Take a magnifying glass and examine the photograph. You will notice that the central set of twisted iron ropes appears to separate from the rest of the picture, giving a three-dimensional impression (emphasized by the magnifying glass). In fact, the ropes are perfectly aligned and parallel to each other, though appearances point to the contrary. The twisted cord illusion is probably due to orientation-sensitive simple cells in the striate cortex in our brains, which interact to combine the closely spaced tilted lines into a single tilted line.

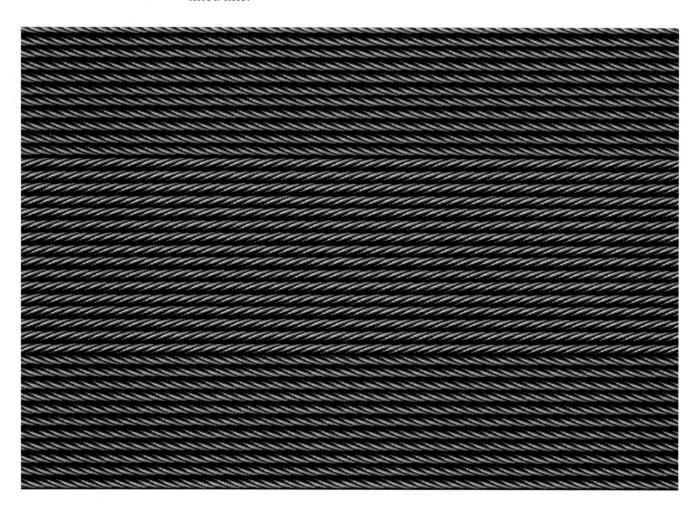

ANAMORPHIC COLOURED CUBES

The background of this room seems transparent, allowing you to see two floating colour cubes. The lower pictures reveal how this trompe l'oeil was created.

Figure A

Figure B

IS THIS BALCONY SAFE?

The Future Condominium is a building in Manhattan – 200 East 32nd Street – designed by architect Costas Kondylis. The balconies appear to slant upward (Fig. A) or downward (Fig. B) depending on one's point of view. As you can see in Fig. C, however, it is the parallelogram shape of the balconies that is causing this illusion.

Figure C

GEOMETRIC NAUSEA

This eerie underground car park might give you goose bumps! All the pillars appear to be distorted and concave (although they are in fact perfectly straight and parallel to each other).

The essential elements that cause the distortion are the black and white dots placed near the borders of each single square of the chequered pattern painted on the pillars. It is as if each of the dots pushes against the border of the square, visually bending it slightly and thus affecting the neighbouring squares and the overall look of the patterns (see Fig. A).

Figure A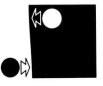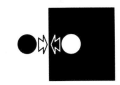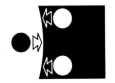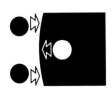

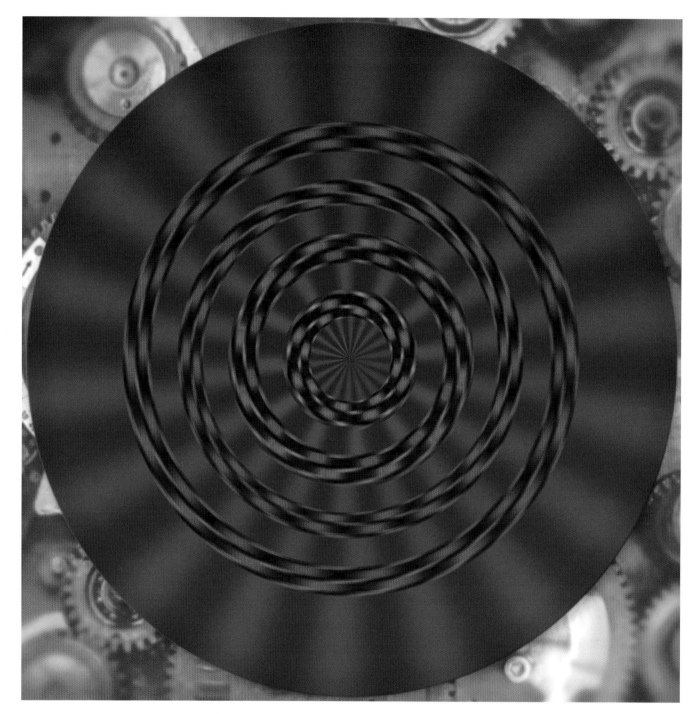

COAXIAL AXIS?

Though the coloured rings seem to be off-centre and even to have curvatures that telescope into one another, they are perfectly circular and have a common axis. Moreover, the rings will seem to counter-rotate when you approach or move away from the picture while concentrating on its centre. All these illusive effects disappear if the image is reduced.

The contrasting angular direction of the patterns within the circular insets is responsible for the illusion, which is similar to the Zöllner illusion.

CRAZY CUBES

Relying on contradictory cues for depth perception, this optical illusion depicting a set of cubes offers many different spatial interpretations. Can you say how many cubes there are in the picture? You may find that this varies according to your angle of view.

Some people are able to perceive four distinct cubes: a large one, a medium and two small ones. In fact, this scene offers visual ambiguities in several ways: a medium cube floating in front of a larger cube; a large cube with a corner cube cut out; seen upside-down, a medium cube resting in the back corner of three perpendicular adjoining planes; and the two smallest volumes can also be seen as two solid cubes or just as two small perpendicular adjoining planes.

MAGIC PILLAR

This photograph, taken in the German town Bad Langensalza, shows one of many pillars placed around a fountain. Is the pillar hollow or does it have a pyramid on top of it?

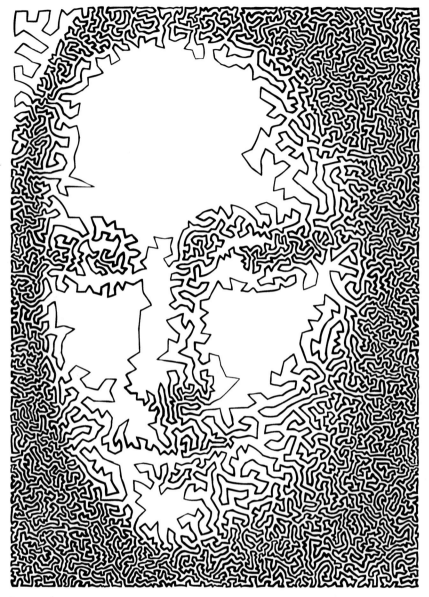

Figure A

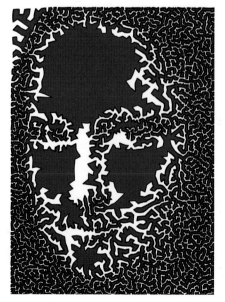

Figure B

PATTERNING MONA

Look carefully at the image of the *Mona Lisa* from a distance. Do you notice something peculiar about it? In this picture, made by a process called TSP Art, Leonardo's famous model is represented entirely by a single non-intersecting path, created automatically by a computer, that wiggles and bends to cover the canvas. The computer covers the original image with points, and then tries to connect the points into a path by solving the 'Travelling Salesman Problem', a famously difficult problem in computer science. The red filling-in of the picture outline (see Fig. B) reveals that it is a kind of Jordan's curve – a curve that is closed and does not intersect itself.

This version of *La Gioconda* by Leonardo da Vinci was created by Craig S. Kaplan, a visual researcher who studies the interactions between computer graphics, art and mathematics. You can find more information on TSP art from the following site: www.oberlin.edu/math/faculty/bosch/making-tspart-page.html

CYLINDRICAL ANAMORPHOSIS

Anamorphosis is a kind of art that distorts an object so that it is only revealed from a single vantage point or from its reflection on a mirrored surface. This artistic process, which involves geometry, was first attempted during the Renaissance and became exceedingly popular during the Victorian era.

In the picture you can see two kinds of cylindrical anamorphosis. The upper picture shows an interesting circular pattern which turns into a set of cubes. The lower picture shows an example of anamorphic comic-book art from OOZ & OZ's Morph-O-Scopes kit, Sports of All Sorts.

CHAPTER 4

AMBIGUOUS ILLUSIONS

'A man who is not a man saw and did not see a bird that was not a bird in a tree that was not a tree; he hit and did not hit it with a stone that was not a stone. What is the answer?'

Plato, *The Republic*

There is an old Indian story about seven blind men deciding what an elephant looked like. The first man felt the elephant's ear and said, 'The elephant is a large leaf'. The second one took hold of the leg and maintained, 'No, the elephant is a tree trunk!' The third man had the tail and said, 'Maybe the elephant is a thick rope.' The fourth man touched the body and said, 'The elephant is a wall.' The fifth fellow held the trunk and countered, 'No, the elephant is a snake!' The sixth man put his hand in the elephant's mouth and said, 'The elephant is just a bag'. The seventh man felt the tusk and said, 'The elephant is a spear'.

All of them were right, in a way, but none of them had the correct picture of an elephant!

This story demonstrates the relative nature of reality and the subjectivity of perception. In fact, the way we see always depends on prior knowledge, context and expectation (we are very suggestible!). Our minds work analogically, that is,

they work by comparison, so they cannot represent the real world accurately and unambiguously.

When an artist notices that one thing can have two different interpretations, or two distinct things may have a similar appearance, and reproduces a picture with such characteristics, he or she creates what we call an image with double meaning. Many great Renaissance and Baroque artists portrayed ambiguous pictures with hidden faces, including Leonardo da Vinci, Albrecht Dürer and Giuseppe Arcimboldo. Surrealist painters revived this style of art in the first part of the 20th century, especially Max Ernst, René Magritte and Salvador Dalí.

In short, ambiguous illusions are pictures or objects that generally present the viewer with a choice of two or more interpretations, each of which may be valid. As you will learn in the following pages, the large family of ambiguous illusions includes ambiguous figures, reversible figures and composite figures.

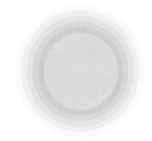

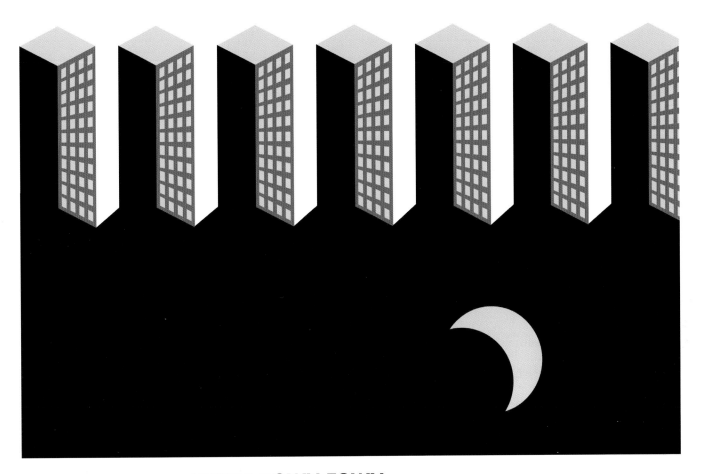

UPSIDE-DOWN-TOWN

Night follows day when the picture is turned upside-down.

HOW MANY ANIMALS?

Is this a sea lion lying on the ice or a polar bear crawling out of a water hole? This bistable optical illusion, created by Gianni A. Sarcone in 1994, has been copied many times, becoming a classic icon in the world of ambiguous illusions. The variant on the right is the most widely disseminated illusion by Sarcone on the internet.

A VERY STRANGE BOX

This strange wrought iron trunk occupies two different spatial positions. Are you looking at it at eye level or from behind and below? If you have difficulty seeing both, the boxes with the pink ball in them will help.

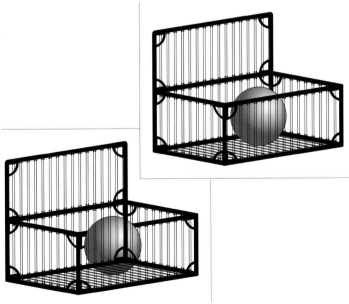

TERRACE DILEMMA...

Which way is the man facing? There are two possible ways to perceive the image: either above (Fig. A) or below (Fig. B) the viewer's eye level. This kind of illusion is known as a bistable or undecidable figure.

Figure A

Figure B

SEAL TO TOUCAN

This topsy-turvy picture transforms a marine mammal into a feathered animal with just a simple turn of the wrist . . . That's magic!

FALSE SIAMESE TWINS

Do these two grave-looking men from another era share the same trunk as if they were conjoined twins? No, of course not, it is just a visual illusion. Baffling, isn't it?

DARK RIDER

Are the rider and his faithful dog moving away to the horizon or towards the viewer? It is impossible to say. This example illustrates how difficult it is to assess the direction of a silhouette or a shaded image.

AMERICAN PRESIDENTS

Look at this portrait from a distance and you'll discover that you can see
Abraham Lincoln in a portrait created from a combination of 42 small portraits
of all the US presidents. This is by Scott Blake, an American artist most well-
known for turning barcodes into Op and Pop art. You can see his website at
www.barcodeart.com

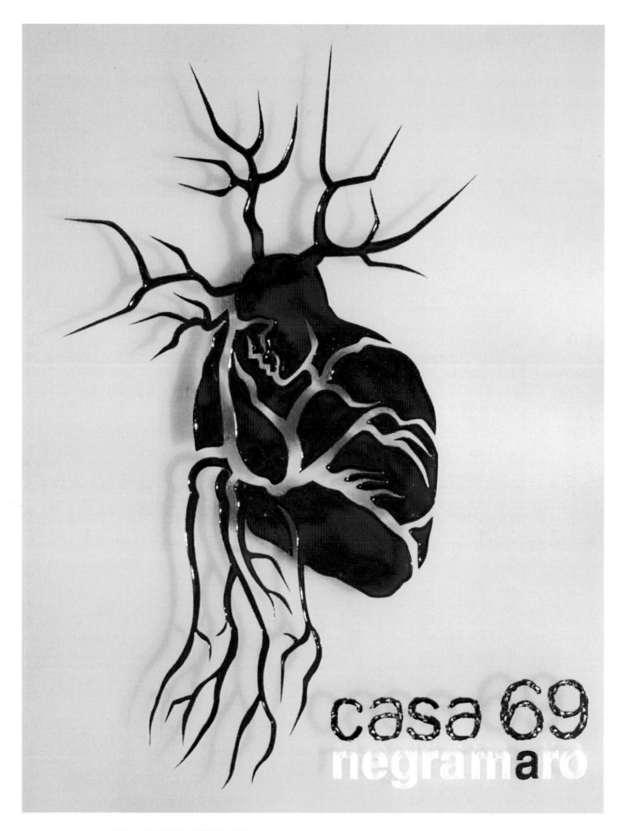

BROKEN HEART

This crimson heart, which appeared on the cover of the album *Casa 69* by the Italian rock group Negramaro, contains a body curled in the foetal position.

MOUNTAIN MAGIC

Look carefully at this Chinese landscape and you
may uncover a mystery – a sleeping face.

RAT/CAT DUPLICITY...

This cat is on the hunt for mice and rats: can you find its prey?

MASK OF LOVE

The picture shows a mask of a pensive person. But is it a woman or a man? Most people who see the picture for the first time do not notice that it is actually both: a woman on the left who is kissing a man on the right. Once the viewer discerns two individual faces, his or her brain will 'flip' between two possible interpretations of the mask. This optical illusion was presented to the public by the authors of this book at the 2011 Best Illusion of the Year Contest. You can see the complete scientific explanation of the illusion along with an animated version online: http://illusioncontest.neuralcorrelate.com/2011/mask-of-love/

TESSELLATED JUDOKAS

In this Escher-esque design, the judokas dressed in white throw their opponents dressed in black (and vice versa). The interlaced martial artists are intended to symbolize the concept of 'yin yang', which describes how polar opposites or seemingly contrary forces are interconnected and interdependent in the natural world.

LEGLESS CROCODILE

The crocodile in this old picture has no legs! Is it genetically modified? No, it is just a matter of playing a game with the reflection.

VERY STRONG PEOPLE!

By distributing printed paper bags in stores, a clever marketing agency turned pedestrians into free outdoor advertisements for Shumensko beer.

PET EYES

Wherever you stand, this dog will always look at you! To understand how the trick works look at the picture showing the top view of this charming three-headed canine. This ambiguous object is a rare and funny Chinese statuette collected by magician Mark Setteducati.

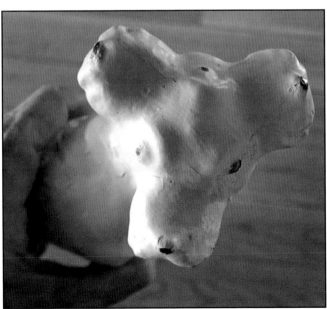

CHAPTER 5

HIDDEN FIGURES

'Finding is just a process of retrieving something that is already there.'

Sigmund Freud

In this chapter we shall play hide and seek with hidden and camouflaged figures. In nature, camouflage is a visual 'noise', usually made from line or dot patterns that enable creatures to blend in with their surroundings and become imperceptible to predators. Since antiquity, human beings too have tried to camouflage themselves or their properties in order to dupe human predators, such as thieves, spies, soldiers and so on.

Some hidden-figure illusions involve the figure-ground phenomenon, which refers to the human ability to separate figures or foreground information from a surrounding background or 'noise', which requires a complicated perceptual process by the brain. What is interesting here is that the main figure and the background share the same contour but the brain considers only one field, neglecting the other

as being a negative space or an interspace.

In psychology, the term 'pregnance' (from the German word *Prägnanz*) is applied to the tendency to distinguish certain objects from their background. Hidden figures are widely used in neuropsychology to assess figure-ground discrimination. These tests are called Embedded Figures Tests (EFT). Those who score highly are described as being 'field-independent', and have the ability to 'distinguish the message from the noise', while those who find it difficult to discern the hidden shapes have a greater tendency to perceive complete patterns rather than their separate components and are called 'field-dependent'.

In the following pages you will find some particular hidden figures that are designed to make the viewer experience a sense of a shifting figure/ground relationship. We hope you will enjoy them!

HALLOWEEN POPCORN

How many spooky skulls can you spot in this bowl
of popcorn? See page 126 for the answer.

LOST ELEPHANTS

Find all the four elephants camouflaged in this chaotic pile of jigsaw-puzzle pieces. Go to page 126 to see if you have got them right.

WHERE IS HER BOYFRIEND?

Find the cowgirl's boyfriend in this picture. Hint: have a look
at the large white blaze on the horse's head.

INVISIBLE SQUARES

How many squares are there in this geometric diagram? When you have found as many as you can, go to page 126 for the answer.

FIND ILLUMINATION

Find the serene countenance of Buddha in the leaves. Don't stress – some people have taken 15 minutes to find it!

GHOST CONTOURS

You can see here the contours of two diamond shapes. They are edged by semi-circular shapes and appear to be brighter than the surrounding area, though they have exactly the same brightness, or reflectance, as the background. This is an interesting variant of the famous subjective contour illusion called the Kanisza triangle.

Figure A

HOW MANY CIRCLES?

How many circles do you see in this colour pattern (Fig. A)? First-time viewers do not usually see the four circles segmented from the background (Fig. B); they are only conscious of a series of rectangles. The illusion pits segmentation cues against what appears to be a very strong priority to interpret the image as a series of decorative patterns with closed boundaries; the two distinct interpretations of squares versus circles compete with each other in the brain for access to conscious perception. This illusion, created by Gianni A. Sarcone, was readapted by researcher Anthony Norcia of Smith-Kettlewell Eye Research Institute, USA, and qualified for the top 10 category in the 2006 Best Visual Illusion of the Year Contest.

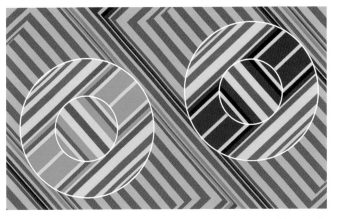

Figure B

ALOHA!

There are two important errors hidden in the image of the hula girl. Your mission is to spot them both! See page 127 for the answer.

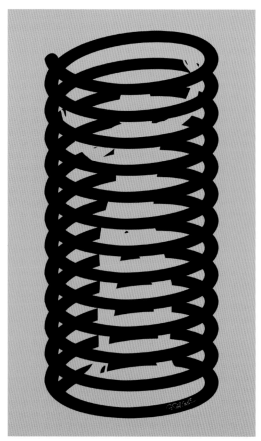

SPRINGS OF LOVE

Though there is no girl in this picture you cannot help seeing the illusory volume and contour of one, appearing to be brighter than the background.

HAND-PRINT ILLUSION

In this hand-print you can see more than just a hand – there is the image of a gorilla in it. Can you spot it?

ELEPHANT WITH A SECRET

Look at this picture from a distance. It is said that elephants are afraid of mice – but not this one. Why not? Hint: just take a magnifying glass and move it around the picture.

THREE-DIMENSIONAL SUBJECTIVE CONTOURS

You may see a spotted spring-like device, but where are its contours?
In fact, such a spring cannot exist because it is formed by floating
coloured discs and semicircles. This is a three-dimensional variant
of the Kanisza triangle contour illusion.

WILD CHILD

A tourist took this photograph of a tiger when travelling in India and noticed afterwards that there was a child camouflaged in the picture. Can you spot him? See page 127 for the answer.

CHAPTER 6

SEEING THE IMPOSSIBLE

'A knife without a blade for which the handle is missing'

G. C. Lichtenberg

In a parallel universe, there is a small town with just one barber. In this town all the men keep themselves clean-shaven, some by shaving themselves, others by visiting the barber. It seems reasonable to imagine that in this strange universe the barber obeys the following rule: 'I must shave all and only those men in town who do not shave themselves'. Under this scenario, we can ask the following question: Who shaves the barber?

The situation presented is in fact impossible: if the barber does not shave himself, he must abide by the rule and shave himself; if he does shave himself, according to the rule he will not shave himself.

In art too it is possible to create paradoxical objects that similarly demolish the foundation of our reality by contradicting themselves. As you will know, art has the ability to represent what cannot exist in reality. Indeed some modern artists are able to accurately represent objects that cannot exist according to the known laws of physics by using pictorial rules

to create the illusion of three dimensions, but then breaking some of these rules to make the objects impossible to construct, conveying a vision of a new and stunning world. Impossible objects belong to the paradoxical 'sphere of neither existing nor non-existing objects'!

While they are fun to look at and ponder over, such impossible objects or figures also reveal important insights into how our mind constructs a three-dimensional percept from a two-dimensional image. Illusionist artists such as M.C. Escher, Oscar Reutersvärd and Jos de Mey were really skilled in tricking the viewer into thinking that their imaginary pictorial structures with ambiguous or incompatible connections in line drawings could be constructed in reality. Some contemporary artists, as Sandro del Prete, Zenon Kulpa, István Orosz, and the authors of this book are also experimenting with impossible figures.

Generally, when a portion of a depicted object conveys conflicting depth or position cues such as ahead/behind, front/back, inward/outward,

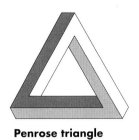

Penrose triangle or tribar

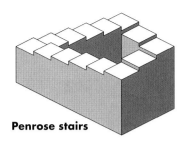

Penrose stairs

above/below or top/bottom, there are chances that you are in presence of an impossible figure, sometimes also described as an 'undecidable figure'. The notable impossible figures known as the Penrose tribar and the Penrose stairs (see above) contain ahead/behind and top/bottom depth-contradictions respectively. Another notable modern impossible figure is the Devil's fork, which appears to have three cylindrical prongs at one end that mysteriously transform into two rectangular prongs at the other end (see page 74). Before the discovery of perspective in the Renaissance, many artists painted what at first sight appear as impossible figures. In fact, scale, distance and perspective were not respected in most medieval paintings. The best-known example in art of an unintentionally impossible object (a gallows!) was painted by Pieter Brueghel in his artwork *Magpie on the Gallows*, 1568 (below). However, the first artist to deliberately misuse perspective in order to create an absurd and impossible landscape was William Hogarth (see page 26).

MY AMBIGUOUS RUST BUCKET

Could you drive such an old car? It would certainly be good for parking in a tight space! The car can be perceived simultaneously from front, side or back.

MAGIC CRAYONS

This man has found a neat way of drawing an impossible tribar – using a three-leaded pencil based on the Devil's fork!

SHAPE OF THE UNREAL

The curious module in the foreground that the inventive engineer has designed can exist only in the fourth dimension, not in the real world.

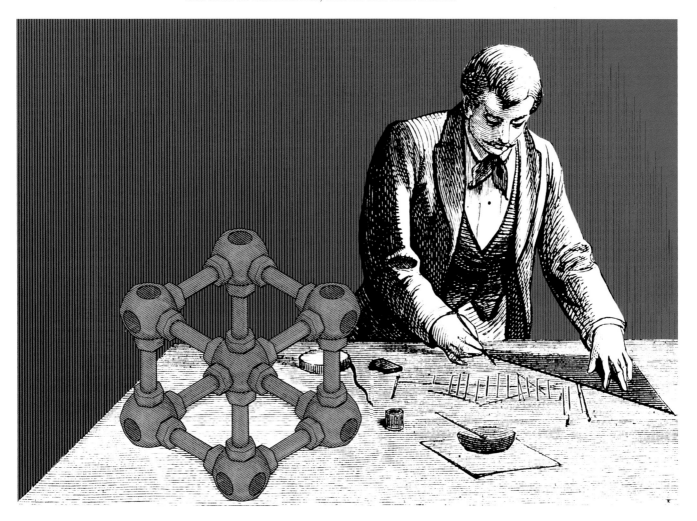

IMPOSSIBLE CONTORTIONS

Here an acrobat is performing on an impossible
ceiling-hung structure.

PRISONER OF MY DREAMS

The bars of the jail on the foreground and the background scenery are blended together. Moreover, a nocturnal dimension appears in the space that divides the vertical bars. The bars are of course impossible objects, acting as surreal props that reveal a dream world. The man staring out through the bars adds an hypnotic feel.

FROM ABOVE AND BELOW

Here an impossible structure is made entirely from cubes.

THE GENOESE WAY

Look at this picture of a *palazzo* in Genoa (Italy). The upper and lower sections of the building seem to share a common side, but that is impossible because the image is actually a blending of two different points of view of the same *palazzo*. The two façades with the portals seem unexpectedly to lean forwards or backwards depending on your angle of view. This illusion is comparable to the 'Thiéry figure', which is a classic ambiguous figure devised by the psychologist Armand Thiéry in the late 19th century.

ORIGAMI MAGIC

This magician has given a performance of impossible paper folding.

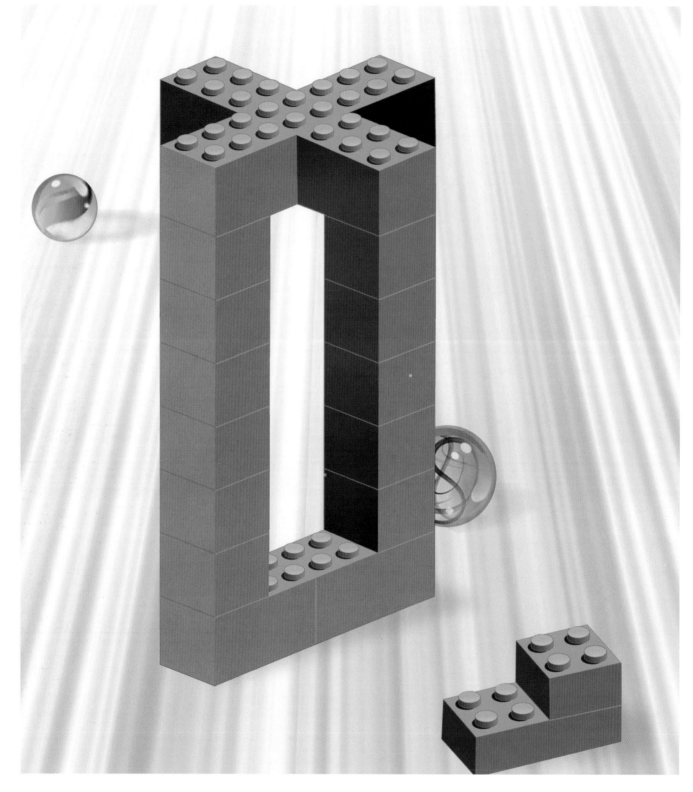

LEGO STRUCTURE

Lego is capable of many things, but here is a structure that no one could ever build.

UN-STAIR

A lucid dream of a distorted world: the platform and stairs form an impossible continuous loop. The girl could walk and climb the stairs forever and never get any higher.

CHAPTER 7

AUTOKINETIC ILLUSIONS

'Eppur si muove' ('And yet it does move . . .'')
Galileo Galilei

Everything moves and everything changes. The Greek philosopher Heraclitus once said: 'There is nothing permanent except change.' Motion is ingrained in life, though some objects move very quickly (such as electrons) and others so slowly (a growing tree, for example) that they seem static.

Seeing a stable world while we are moving (which we do all the time without being aware of it) requires such elaborate visual compensations that sometimes something in the process goes wrong. For instance, when a stationary small and dim light such as a lit cigarette is observed for several minutes in a very dark room it seems to move and swing around, usually in a fairly random path. This is due to small movements of the eyes called 'saccades' that are not monitored by the brain. Everyone experiences some eye drifting, or saccades, because it is very demanding for the eyes to maintain a steady and accurate gaze when you look at an object.

In the world of optical illusions, the terms 'autokinetic illusion' or 'apparent motion' are used to describe the convincing appearance of movement in a picture that the viewer knows to be static. This particular form of visual trickery has a long history. The Ancient Romans were aware of how to create the illusion of movement, applying their knowledge of optics and perspective to create amazing illusive mosaic floors that fool the eye into thinking they are rotating slightly. During the 1960s, the Op Art (short for Optic Art) movement – the leaders of which were Victor Vasarely, Richard Anuszkiewicz and Bridget Riley – began experimenting with new visual concepts designed to trick the eye and stimulate the brain. Op Art paintings and exhibits play with interferences and moiré effects to create illusory colours and to simulate motion. Recently, new classes of autokinetic illusions have been created, notably by Akiyoshi Kitaoka, Baingio Pinna and the authors of this book.

There is an ongoing debate about what generates the illusion of movement in our visual system, and a number of conflicting theories. Opposite are some possible causes.

WHAT KIND OF DESIGN CREATES SUCH ILLUSIONS?

1 The main anomalous or relative motion illusions are based on repetitive patterns that alternate optical contrasts (clear/dark, vertical/horizontal, left/right, straight/oblique, thick/thin, and so on).
2 Colour luminance contributes strongly to increasing the relative motion effects.
3 When two grids are overlaid at an angle, or when they have slightly different mesh sizes, they produce interesting visual vibrating sensations. Such grids are known as 'interference patterns', or 'moirés'.

WHICH PART OF OUR VISUAL SYSTEM IS AFFECTED?

1 Momentary pauses in luminance processing produce a signal that tricks the motion system. The areas V1 and V5 of the visual cortex are involved in this process.
2 Some autokinetic illusions are more easily seen when the gaze is not directly concentrated upon them. Most observers see the illusion when reading text with the illusion figure in the periphery.
3 Random eye saccades; our visual system does not monitor the saccade movements of the eye, so the brain thinks the image rather than the eye is moving.
4 Lateral inhibition is caused by each group of photoreceptors on the eye's retina tending to inhibit the response of the one next to it. While this increases contrast and sharpness of vision, it can also have the effect of creating large dark patches at the intersection of a grid.
5 Afterimage effects may overlap the actual image, creating a visual swarming.

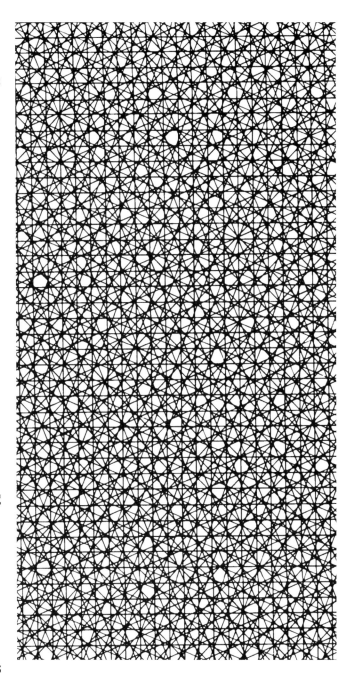

If you look at this autokinetic drawing – based on the work called 'Tirets' by the French Op Art artist François Morellet – small circles will appear to scintillate and fade intermittently.

Figure A

HYPNOTIC VIBES

Don't stare at this vibrating optical illusion (Fig. A) for too long or it might hypnotize you! This illusion, created by Gianni A. Sarcone, was selected for the advertising campaign of the eye drop Alfa Protezione UV (Fig. B).

Figure B

VORTEX

This colourful radial pattern seems to rotate and expand slightly. The central disc moves independently from the surrounding beams and seems to levitate.

TIME EXPANSION

This star-like pattern appears to vibrate, flicker and expand. If you move your head backwards and forwards while focusing on the watch, the pattern will give the impression of bulging.

GHOST IMAGES

Do you perceive bright 'ghost' blobs or smudges at the intersections of the lines? There are many explanations and counter-explanations regarding this illusion, which is related to the Hermann grid illusion. The illusory effect disappears if you look at the picture from a distance or too closely.

MAGNETIC TUNNEL

The colour fields of this 'magnetic' rosette appear to vibrate when you move your head backwards and forwards, keeping the focus on the ball at the centre of the image; the colour fields move forwards as if you were in a warp tunnel. This illusion involves colour contrast and dynamic luminance-gradient effects.

DEADLY DAZZLES

What a dazzling pattern! The repetitive arrangement of contrasting lines and the eye saccades are responsible for the uncomfortable visual oscillations you may experience when watching this picture. In addition, the image of a skull is encrypted in the geometric pattern – can you spot it?

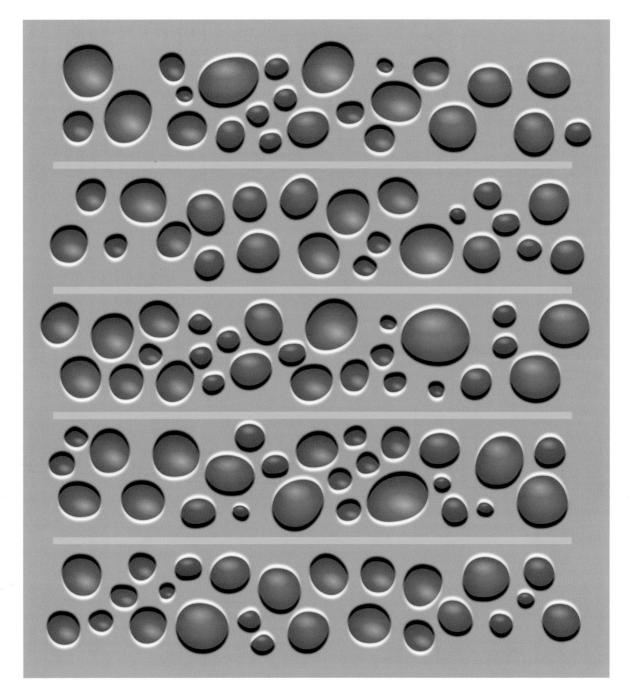

WAVING LINES

Here the water drops seem to move slightly up and down and the yellow horizontal lines appear to wave and wobble! Curiously enough, vision researchers have demonstrated that illusory motion triggers brain areas similar to those activated by real motion.

E-MOTION

As you sweep your gaze around the picture, the small red hearts appear to move diagonally in two opposite directions, while the large blue heart seems to pulsate slightly. The shaded tones and the contrasting black and white edges of the small hearts induce a shifting in the retinal image when your eyes move, activating motion-sensitive neurons in your brain. This activation is incorrectly translated as real motion.

ARITHMETICAL PERPETUAL MOTION

The wheel looks as if it is rotating! This perpetual motion device works thanks to the rotational symmetry that transforms a 6 into a 9, and vice versa. The apparent motion of the wheel is mainly due to the colour and light contrasts of the disc. It occurs in the peripheral vision – if you gaze steadily at the wheel it will be stationary.

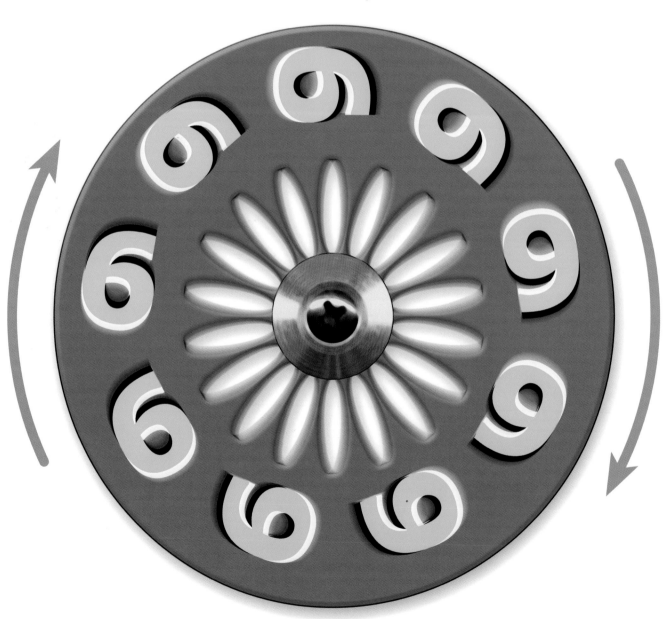

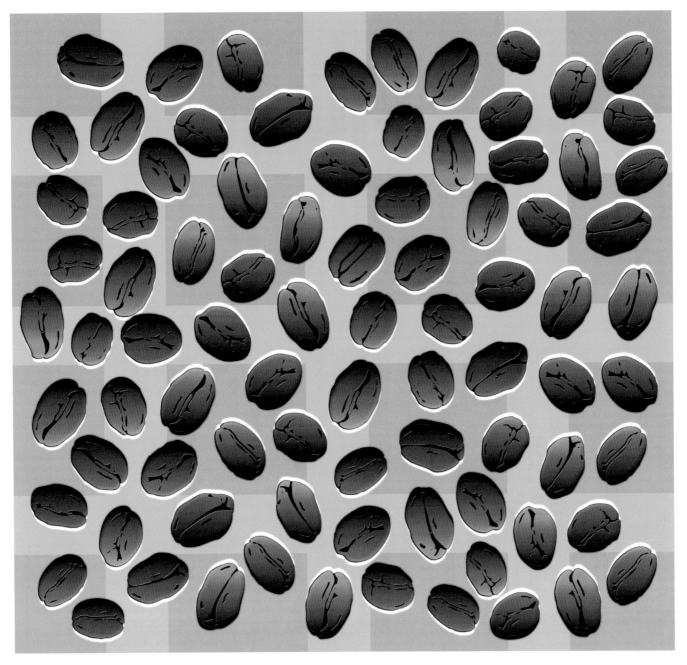

MEXICAN JUMPING COFFEE BEANS

Colour and brightness sometimes induce apparent motion effects in the peripheral vision as you move your gaze around. Though the image is completely still, the coffee beans seem to move!

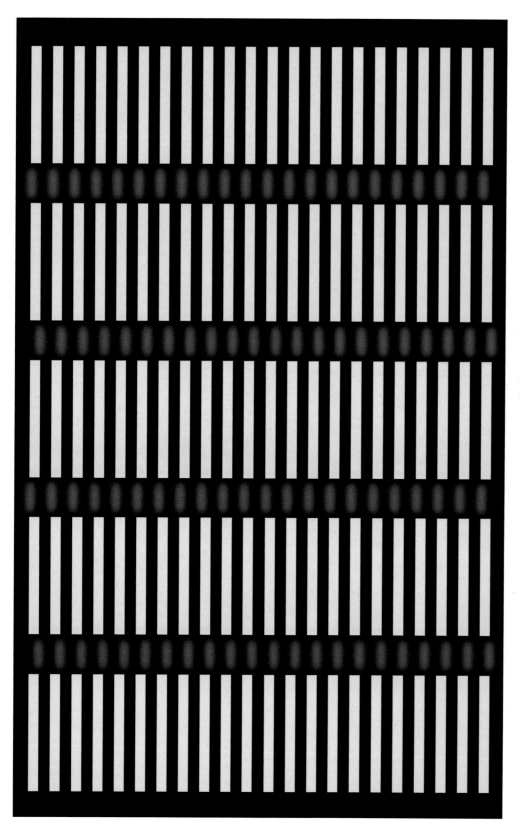

TO AND FRO FLOWS

Sandwiched between the yellow rods, the alignments of purple blurs seem intermittently to brighten and deepen, creating an unending animation of illusory back and forth flows.

MOVING WHEELS

If you move your eyes around the page the wheels will appear to rotate slightly. This peripheral drift illusion is perfect for web pages and desktop wallpapers.

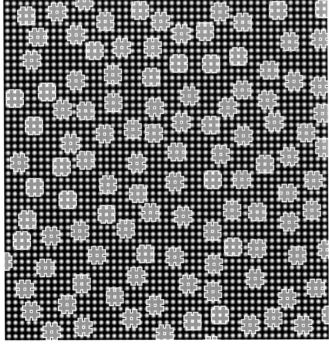

OBSERVATION TEST

Look at this picture for a while; the colour designs will seem to slightly float and move over the dark background. Most people believe there are two or three types of pattern, but in fact there is only one; the floating patterns look different because the regularity of their shape is disturbed by the background.

CHAPTER 8

VISUAL DISTORTIONS

*'A thing is mighty big when time and distance
cannot shrink it'*

Zora Neale Hurston

Our binocular vision – that is, the sense of sight that is given by two eyes with overlapping fields of view – allows for good perception of depth. Usually, our eyes converge to focus on an object, which means that each eye records a different angle of the visual field to create a stereo vision in our brain (binocular disparity).

In the real world we rarely misjudge distances or sizes, or see curvatures where there are only straight lines. Most size misperception or shape distortion illusions stem from the fact that we look at a two-dimensional (flat) object (for instance, any of the illusions printed in this book) as if we were looking at a three-dimensional one; we always see in perspective, even when we look at a flat picture or photograph. So, we estimate things not as they actually appear, but as we imagine them in a converging perspectival space, such as a real landscape. When we visually compare two objects, our cognitive system applies the 'law of size constancy', which states that between two similarly shaped objects distributed in our visual space, the one with a larger relative size is perspectively perceived as closer; and between two objects of relative equal size, the one that appears more distant is sensed as taller.

Also, many perplexing distortion illusions take their source from the twisted cord illusion. This type of illusion is so named because it resembles a cable with twisted threads and consists basically of an alignment of vertical lines or bars each containing a stack of small oblique segments of alternating colours, generally in black and white (see right). The overall effect of these tilted segments is an apparent slanting of the whole contour. Twisted cord illusions are still the subject of considerable theoretical interest and investigation.

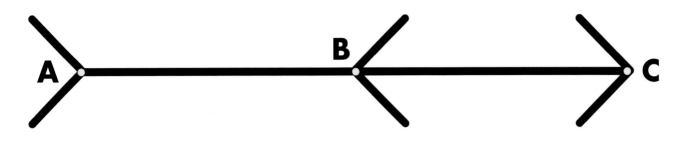

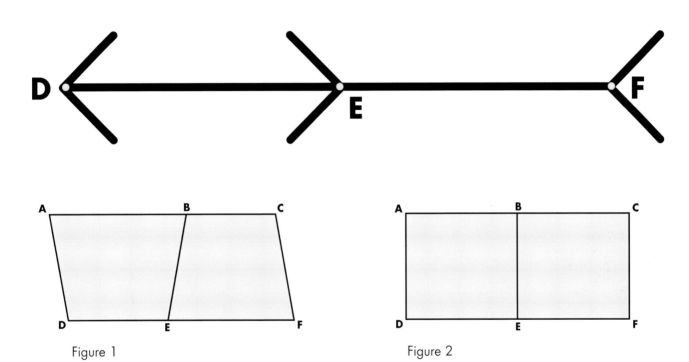

Figure 1   Figure 2

MISLEADING ANGLE BRACKETS

In your imagination, join point A with D, point B with E, and point C with F. Which geometric shape best corresponds to your virtual construction: Fig. 1 or Fig. 2? The vast majority of people choose the former. In fact, segments AB, BC, DE and EF are all equal to each other, so it follows that AD, BE and CF are perpendicular to AC and DF so the right answer is Fig. 2. This illusion is related to the classic Müller-Lyer illusion, where two segments of equal length do not seem the same when 'framed' by angle brackets with the spikes towards the inside or the outside.

DRUNKEN LINES

The horizontal red lines seem wonky and wavy, yet they are perfectly straight and parallel to each other! This is a neat variant of the café wall illusion, originally called the kindergarten illusion in the late 19th century.

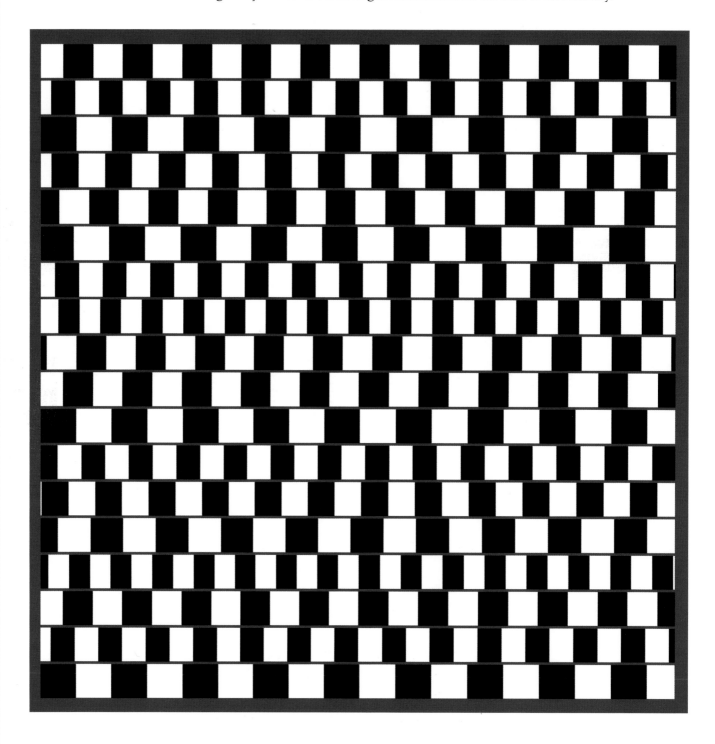

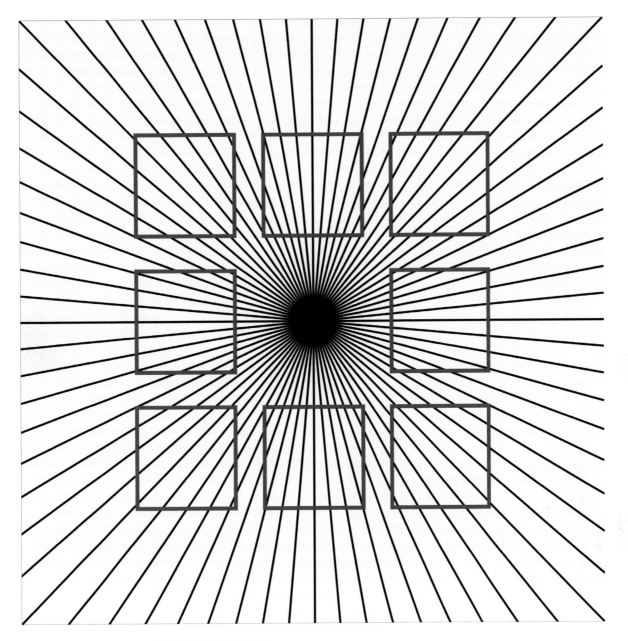

UNSQUARES

These red geometric shapes look like distorted squares of different sizes, but in fact they are all the same size and are perfectly right-angled squares. The visual distortion is caused by the radial spokes in the background, which intersect the sides of the squares at an obtuse angle, giving the viewer the impression there is some sort of perspective. This effect was first described by psychologist William Orbison in 1939.

HUBCAP PUZZLE

Take a careful look at the colour lines across the two ellipses which represent the hubcaps of the tractor. Which line is actually the longest: the red one or the blue one? See page 127 for the answer.

VERTIGO PATTERNS

Do you feel queasy when you look at this wallpaper? Though they appear to be sloped, the columns of stacked white and black patterns are perfectly parallel to each other. This illusion is similar to the café wall illusion.

'SNAKE' CHARMER

As if charmed by music, magic ropes spring out from baskets and rise into the air, writhing like snakes. But are the coloured ropes in the picture really contorted? No, they are perfectly straight and parallel to each other. It is the pattern of tilted elements inside the ropes that generates these interesting curvature effects.

WINE BARREL PUZZLE

Here is an oenological illusion. Which arc, the blue or the green one, is perfectly collinear with the circular contour of the wine barrel (highlighted in red)? See page 127 for the answer.

TABLETOP ILLUSION

It may be hard to believe, but these two tabletops are exactly identical in size and shape. This illusion is based on Roger Shepard's Turning the Tables illusion, first published in 1981.

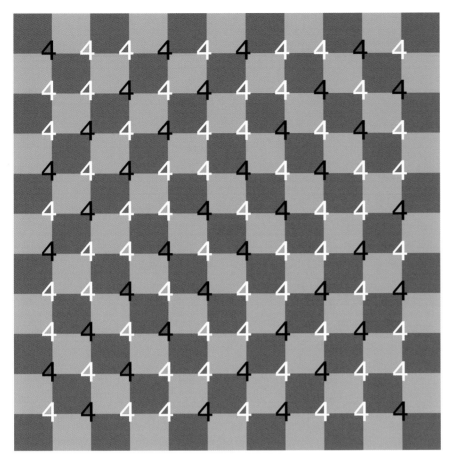

DISTORTION BY NUMBERS

A clever distribution of alternating black and white numbers on a chequered surface can induce interesting visual distortions: the blue checkered square appears to wave, while the orange one seems to shrink towards its centre.

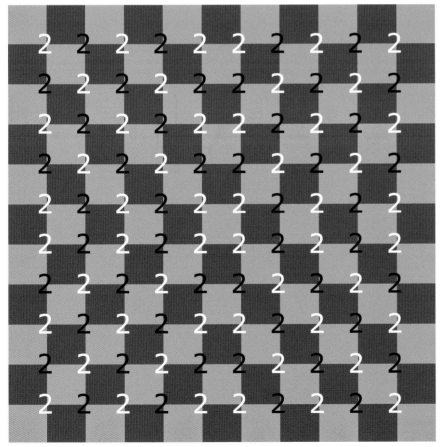

ALIGNMENTS

The five cylinders seem to meet at a single vanishing point in space. Can you find in the drawing any segments that are perfectly collinear (lying in the same straight line)? See page 128 for the answer.

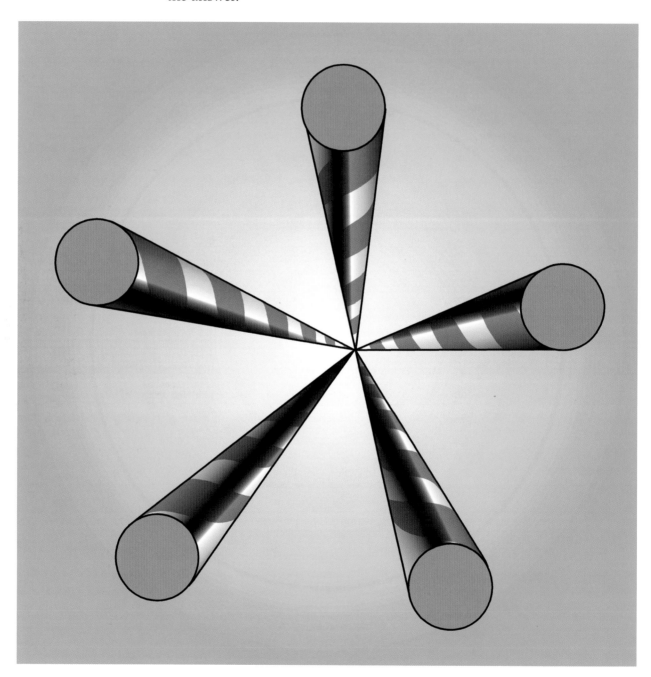

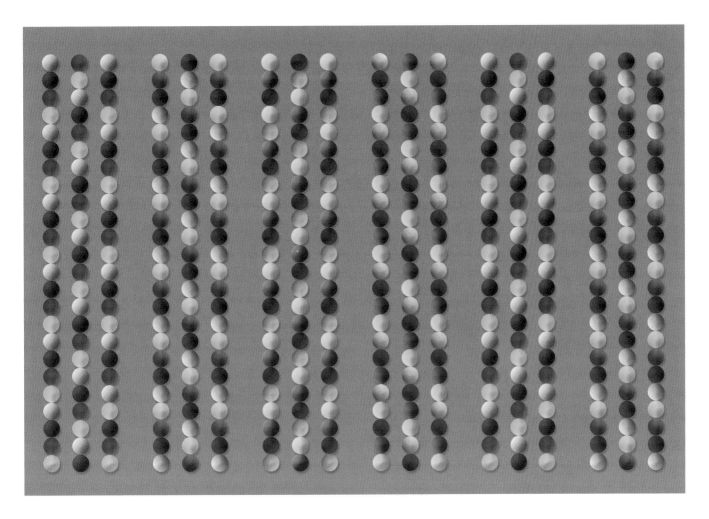

BAFFLING BEADS

These sets of beads appear to tilt, but each single vertical alignment of beads is perfectly parallel. This illusion is based on the twisted cord illusion: in each set of three vertical alignments of beads, beads of the same colour form a diagonal. The combination of all these diagonals makes the sets of beads appear to tilt.

BACKGROUND VERSUS FOREGROUND

A patterned background strongly influences the appearance of foreground lines and shapes. In both pictures all the coloured diagonal lines are straight and parallel to each other; the impression of their curvature is strongest near the focal points of the radiating lines and the axes of the concentric circles.

SNAIL SHELL PUZZLE

This snail shell looks like a spiral, but the recurring pattern is actually made up of concentric ellipses. You don't believe it? Use your forefinger to help guide your eye around any of the ellipses.

BOTANIC ILLUSION

Although these lines appear to diverge, they are perfectly straight and parallel. It is the oblique arrangement of leaves in the background that causes the tilting effect.

CHAPTER 9

CHROMATIC ILLUSIONS

'People can have the Model T in any color, so long as it's black.'
Henry Ford

The concept of colour is confusing for most people, and whether black and white are actually colours at all remains one of the most debated issues. From a scientist you will get a reply based on physics: 'Black is not a colour, white is!', while from an artist you will get another, based on empirical experience: 'Black is a colour, white is not!'

To represent all the visible colours, the 'colour wheel' (Fig. A) is used. Unfortunately, this model is not an accurate representation of reality: a colour spectrum (Fig. B) cannot actually be laid out in a circle, because it has a clear beginning (red) and end (violet). In the colour wheel, the red transforms smoothly and continuously to violet, creating an in-between purplish red colour called magenta, which is a physical contradiction: such a colour is missing from the real colour spectrum.

Colours are an illusory subjective sensation, not an external reality. They change according to their surroundings, so that colours which are identical may appear to be different under certain conditions, and colours that are different may look the same. This effect is called 'colour induction', of which there are two main types.

Of these, 'simultaneous colour contrast' (Fig. C) occurs when the difference between colours that are opposite on the wheel is enhanced by their juxtaposition – for example, greens look greener when placed against red or violet. On the same basis, a grey area tends to look greenish when set against a red background, but will appear reddish against a green background.

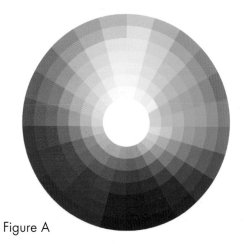

Figure A

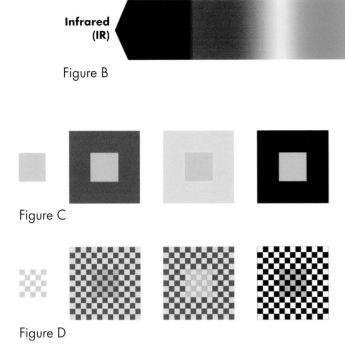

Infrared
(IR)

Ultraviolet
(UV)

Figure B

Figure C

Figure D

a white T-shirt will subjectively look the same whether it is brightly lit on a sunny day or dimly lit on an overcast day, despite the fact that the wavelength of light that reaches the retinas in each case is different. This colour constancy is explained by the fact that the brightness of an object's surroundings usually changes in proportion to the change in brightness of the object itself. Colour constancy is thought to involve specialized neurons in the primary visual cortex.

Most colour illusions shown in this book are due to a specific capacity of our visual system called 'lateral inhibition', which automatically enhances the contrast and sharpness in the images seen. The 'outputs' of this system signal to the brain the location where strong changes in brightness occur even when there are unexpected changes in external light, such as sunlight or day to night transition.

'Colour assimilation' (Fig. D) is the opposite of colour contrast: colours take on the hue of the surrounding colours. For instance, small blue areas tend to look greenish against a yellow background. While the mechanisms of colour contrast phenomena are well understood, how and when colour assimilation occurs is still not completely explained.

In our everyday life, colour influences how we dress, what we eat and the rooms we live in, so it is very important for us to perceive its quality as constant even under changing conditions. For instance, someone travelling in a vehicle with blue-tinted windows will at first see the landscape as suffused with a blue cast, but as the eye quickly desensitizes itself to blue the view will soon reassume its normal coloration. This tendency of the eye to adapt in seconds to most prevailing light sources is called 'colour adaptation' (Fig. E). Thanks to this effect, the eye can accurately identify the colours of objects under changing lighting conditions. For example,

Figure E
Stare at the X in the right-hand diagram for 30 seconds, then look at the duck. What happens?

DARK AND LIGHT STRIPES

Although they look quite different, the broad colour stripes on the outer edges of the picture have exactly the same hue and brightness. This illusion was discovered by Gianni A. Sarcone.

BIG BROTHER

View the picture from a good distance. Do you see an eye with a bright halo around it? Actually, there is no halo at all: the apparent bluish tint is nothing more than a construct of your mind.

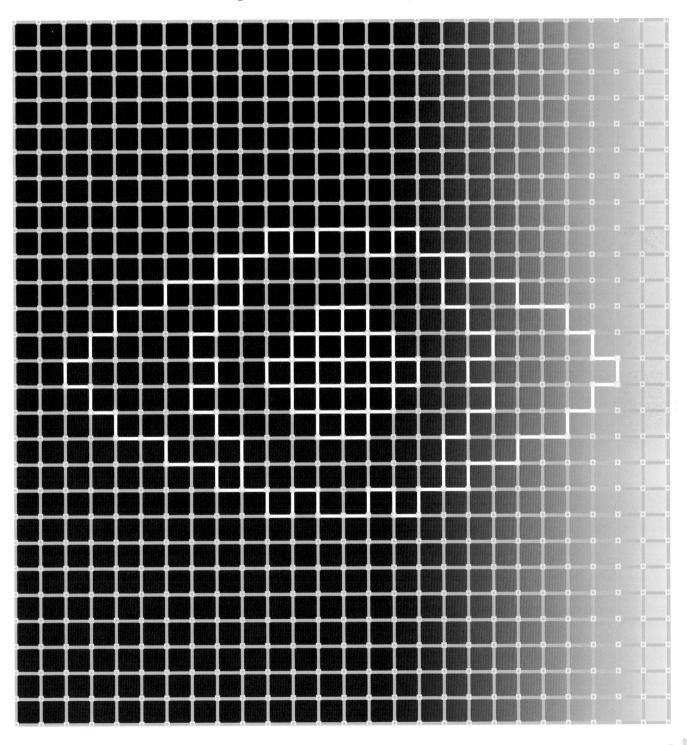

ILLUSORY COLOURS

How many colours do you see in this picture, which represents a pond containing floating waterlily flowers and pads? For the answer, see page 128.

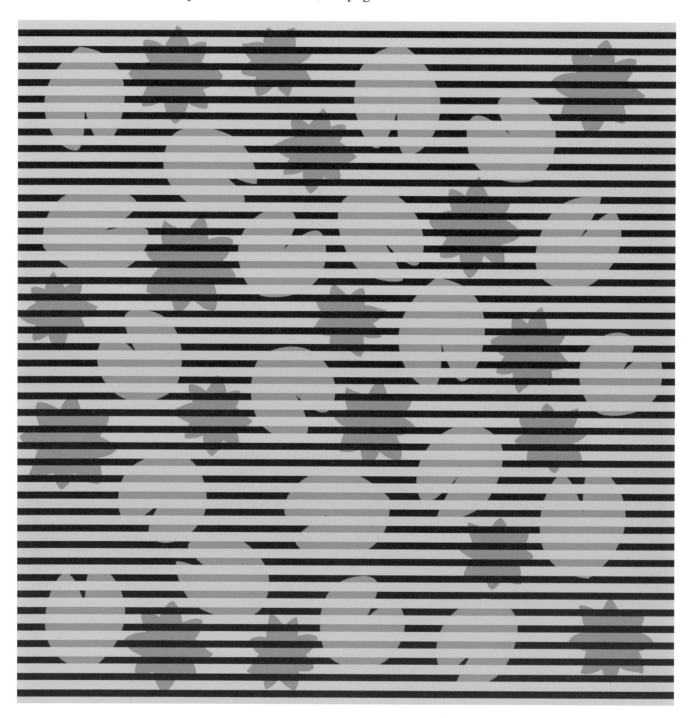

Figure A

Figure B

S. KOREAN FLAG

In honour of South Korea, which has provided many martial arts to the Western world, we can see on the flag two hexagons: one set on the red background of the colour disc, and the other on the blue background (Fig. A). Are the hexagons the same colour? It may not look like they are but you can see from Fig. B that this is the case. This is an example of simultaneous colour contrast.

GRADIENT CAMOUFLAGE

Notice how the same arrangement of dots filled with a gradient hue looks different when it is laid on a background of sand ripples. Some dots become more apparent while others become quite invisible, though all have exactly the same gradient and hue. Gradient-gradient illusions are very common in nature; most animals display a gradient camouflage to blend in with the surrounding environment. Gradient colours instead of solid colours in camouflage patterns would greatly enhance the camouflage effectiveness of military uniforms!

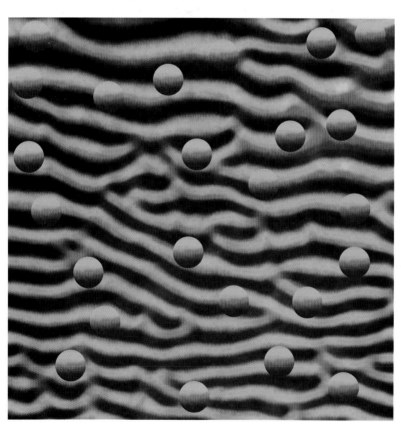

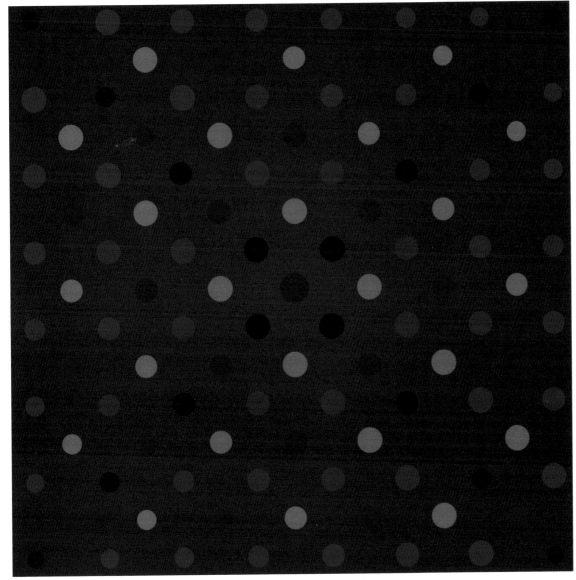

Figure A

NON-EXISTENT GREEN

The green colour that fills some dots in the picture (Fig. A) does not exist – if the colour background is removed, those dots are almost solid black (Fig. B). The emergence of the green colour is induced by the background and the neighbouring shaded dots.

Figure B

117

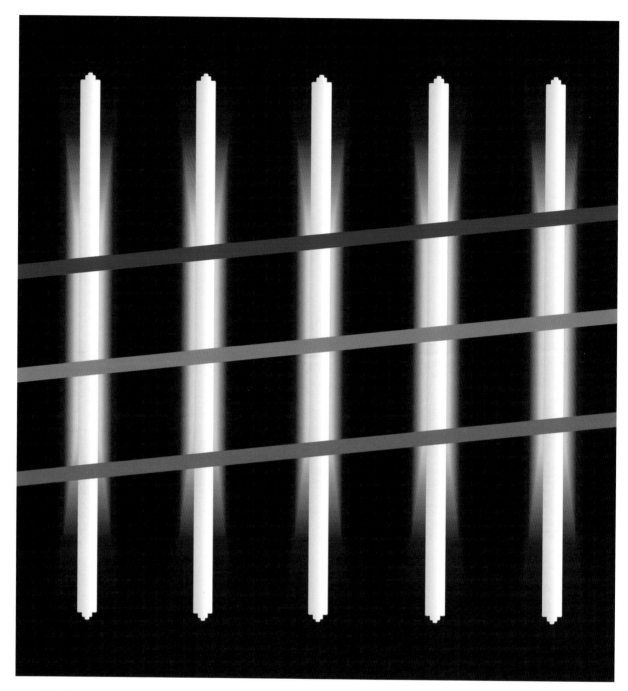

NEON NUANCES

The colour stripes seem to float over the neon tubes shown here. The intermittent dark smudges on the stripes do not exist – this illusion is caused by lateral inhibition, which enhances the contrast of the outline of an object.

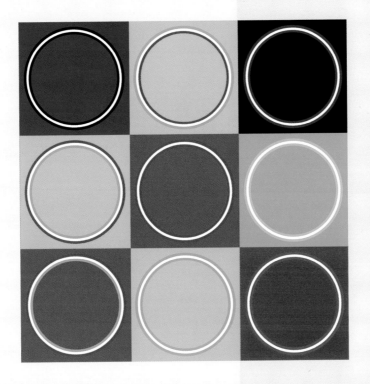

GHOST COLOURS

Look at the coloured rings from a distance and guess which of them are lined inside with yellow and which are lined with sky-blue.

Ninety per cent of people given this test answer that the first and second column of rings contain yellow and the third one contains a blue tint. In fact it is a trick question: the light tint inside all the rings is just white.

CAT'S EYES

It looks like this cat has green eyes. Actually, only one eye is green – the other one is shown in black and white but seems tinted because of the purple context. Thanks to a mechanism of colour adaptation, the brain desensitizes itself to the purple veil which covers the right side of the cat's face and by doing that it subtracts a bit of purple from the gray eye, which then becomes yellowish-green.

TONAL ILLUSION

Which ball corresponds exactly to ball A – ball B or ball C? The answer is ball C,
even if it seems darker than ball A. This is a simultaneous lightness contrast effect.

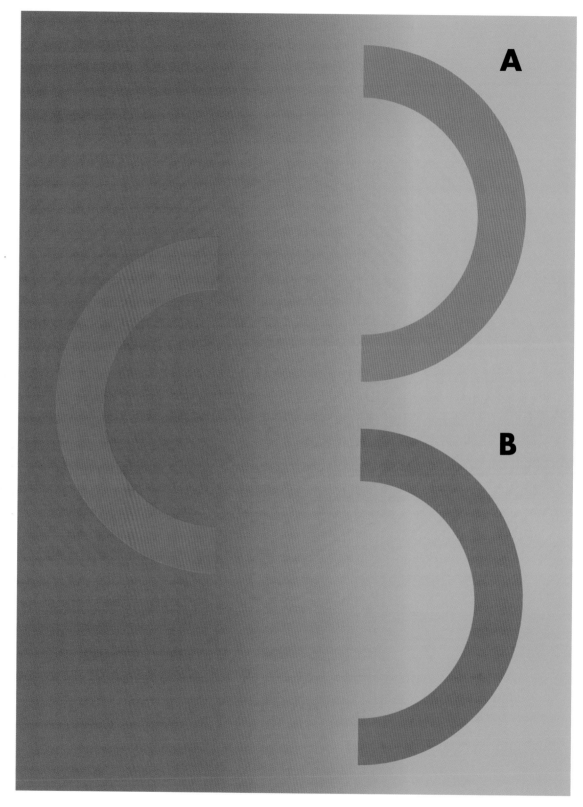

CONFUSING CURVES

Which curved shape (A or B) corresponds to the curve lying on the red background? The answer is B. This illusion, based on the simultaneous colour contrast effect, is a neat variant of the Koffka ring illusion.

GHOST BEAMS

If you sweep your gaze around this picture for a while
you may see intermittent blue radial beams followed by
yellowish beams. Both effects are a construct of your eye
and mind: the first effect is due to the spreading property
of colours and the second one to an afterimage effect.

Figure A

Figure B

TINTS AND BACKGROUNDS

You can see three distinctly tinted colour samples in the picture (Fig. A), but when they are placed on the multicoloured background (Fig. B) the distinction seems to diminish dramatically. This colour experiment shows that different tints can be more difficult to distinguish on a coloured background than on a uniform background.

ALIGNED DOTS?

Your eyes see something different, but all the floating marbles here are the same shade of pink and the ones that appear clearer are perfectly aligned with those which seem darker. These illusions are created by two factors; the contrast of colours and the curved coloured lines.

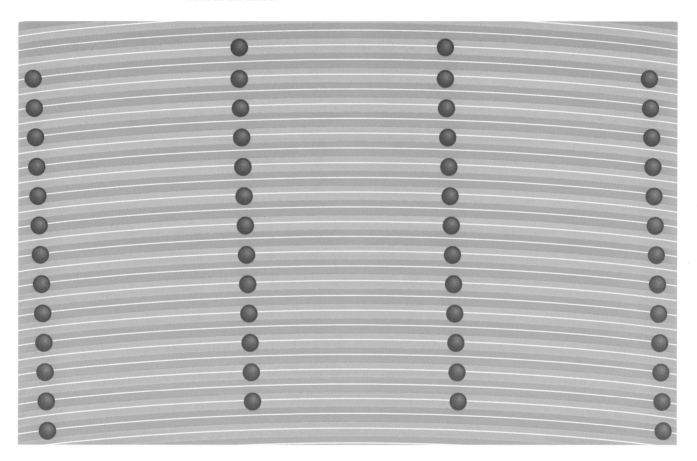

SOLUTIONS

WHERE IS THE DRIVER? *page 29*

HALLOWEEN POPCORN *page 61*

There are at least seven skulls among the popcorn!

LOST ELEPHANTS *page 62*

Did you manage to spot the elephants?
Here, circled in red, they are easy to see.

INVISIBLE SQUARES *page 64*

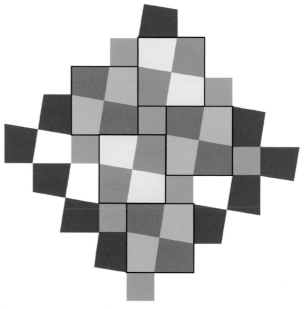

There are 13 perfect squares in the picture!
Did you manage to discover all of them?

ALOHA! *page 68*

The hula girl has two right feet and five fingers on her left hand (plus the concealed thumb).

WILD CHILD *page 71*

The camouflaged profile of the child is on the tiger's cheek.

HUBCAP PUZZLE *page 100*

Eighty per cent of people polled say the red line is longer, but in fact it is shorter than the blue one. There are two factors that strongly influence the brain and cause it to arrive at the wrong answer: the context (the larger ellipse must mean the longest line), and distance (given two same relative lengths, the furthest will always be perceived as the greater). This relative size perception illusion, known as Sarcone's ellipses, was first described by Gianni A. Sarcone in 1997.

WINE BARREL PUZZLE *page 103*

Seventy-five per cent of people who try this test answer that it is the blue arc that is collinear with the wine barrel. The correct answer is the green arc.

ALIGNMENTS *page 106*

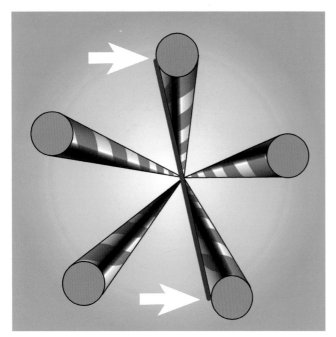

The segments that outline the cylinders all seem to meet at an angle, but there are two segments that are perfectly collinear.

ILLUSORY COLOURS *page 114*

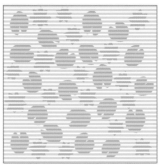

Excluding the background colour, which is purple, there are only two colours: yellow (lines) and blue/cyan (water lilies). There is no green at all in the picture. This illusory colour effect is based on the principle of colour assimilation.

CREDITS

The authors would like to thank the following contributors to this book:

Pages 14 and 15: Scale model illusions © Greg Keene

Page 22: Giovanni Battista Piranesi, 'Arco Gotico', 1778.

Page 35: Ames Room © Piotrek. EXPERYMENT Science Centre, Pomeranian Science and Technology Park, Al. Zwyciestwa 96/98, 81-451 Gdynia, Poland.

Page 37: Anamorphic cubes, Alexis Facca. www.paperdonut.com

Page 41: Magic pillar. Thanks to Prashanth Mahagaonkar

Page 42: Craig S. Kaplan, 'Mona Lisa TSP'.

Page 51: Scott Blake, 'American Presidents'. www.barcodeart.com

Page 56: Tessellated figures, Alain Nicolas, 'Parcelles d'Infini', Edition pour la science, 2005. http://parcellesdinfinifree.fr

Page 58: Schumensko Bag (Carlsberg Bulgaria/Shumensko Beer, May 2008). Photographer Atanas Kanchev, Noble Graphics Creative Studio, Bulgaria, www.noblegraphics.eu

Page 59: Three-headed dog, Mark Setteducati, www.marksetteducati.com